Bishop Auckland Past & Present

by Tom Hutchinson

Multi-view postcard showing two views of Newgate Street, Bondgate (Street), South Road and entrance to Bishop's Park. From 12 Leopold Place in Bishop to Miss E.M. Haw, Rosebank, Woodlands Road, Darlington, posted on 11 August 1924. The message: "Dear Edna, I went to church twice on Sunday. I am enjoying myself immensely. Love and kisses from Lilah. P. S. Had tea in garden twice."

Previous page: Plenty of activity in the Market Place, c. 1920s. It's the message on the reverse which is most interesting – "This is our market place. Markets are held here every Thursday and Saturday. The building behind with clock in tower is town hall and next to it is St. Anne's Church. Many people were married here since it was built and it was discovered in 1908 that it was never licensed for marriages, but parliament declared them all legal." Signed E.J.Kirby. Well, I never! To whom was the postcard sent?

Front cover, top: The middle of the afternoon on market day with pedestrians and motor and horse traffic uncomfortably too close to each other at times. Town Hall and St. Anne's Church are in the background. (c. Beamish Museum).

Bottom: Today – much quieter.

Copyright Tom Hutchinson 2015

First published in 2015 by

Summerhill Books
PO Box 1210, Newcastle upon Tyne NE99 4AH

www.summerhillbooks.co.uk

email: summerhillbooks@yahoo.co.uk

ISBN: 978-1-906721-04-6

No part of this publication may be reproduced, stored in a mechanical retrieval system, or transmitted, in any form or by any means, electronic, mechanical, photocopying, recording or otherwise, without prior permission of the author.

Contents

Then & Now Market Place & Newgate Street	5
Then & Now – Round the Town including South Church	16
Interesting Items including Gone, but Not Forgotten	44
Railways in Bishop Auckland	62
Demolition & Reconstruction	70
Memories & Mementoes	81
Ancient & Modern	85
Bibliography & Acknowledgements	88

The dawn of photography – corner of Market Place and Wear Chare, c. 1870. Thomas Robson was the landlord of the Sportsman Inn and William Stevens landlord of the Eagle Tavern at the 1871 census.

Introduction

In my last book on Bishop Auckland – Bishop Auckland Past Times – published in 2012 there was a section called 'Then & Now' showing the Market Place and Newgate Street in the past, up to 100 years ago, and 2012. The changes were described in the captions as well as in the illustrations. This book is an attempt to show more of the town through time as well as including more pictures of the Market Place and Newgate Street. In addition, many parts of the town experienced dramatic changes in the 1980s and 1990s – from the disappearance of many of the railway facilities, the building of new roads through the town and the by-pass, and the change of use of the railway viaduct. Fortunately, I have been loaned photographs taken in the 1960s before many changes occurred, and the late Ian McClen took many coloured photographs of the demolition and re-construction that took place in the ten or so years from 1983. However, some landmarks did disappear earlier such as the footbridge and wishing temple in the Bishop's Park and some buildings on the north side of the Market Place. For other buildings there was change of use – the closure of Doggarts in 1981 being one that many older people remember. In recent years the establishment of the retail park at Tindale Crescent has meant a drain of the retail functions of the town to that area with the establishment of four big supermarkets and other outlets such as Marks & Spencer. The two supermarkets near the railway station and on the old Wilson's forge site have stabilized the retail function at the south end of Newgate Street, but the Market Place and the north end of Newgate Street have suffered a decline in activity and prosperity in the past 20 years. Hopefully, the planned developments at Auckland Castle and Flatts Farm will arrest that decline. Time will tell, but one has to remain optimistic!

Another multi-view card posted on 12 July 1928 from Bishop Auckland to Miss Gibbs, 57 High Street, Portland, Dorset. The message is: "Dear Hattie. Thanks for letter on Monday. Mrs Teak and I are just getting tea where I have marked X. The rest are on the tennis courts. It is very hot – we are fortunate and getting a lovely time. Grace sends her love to June. I hope Mrs C. gets home today. We were on the sands yesterday. Everything is O.K. I think we are going to Durham tomorrow. Hope Harold and Bert are getting a good time. With love, from Ethel." The 'X' is located above the King's Restaurant. More traditional views on this postcard – Dam Head, War Memorial, Castle, Newgate Street and Market. These views and those on page 2 – any changes? We'll look at many of them later in the book.

Then & Now

Some of the oldest houses in the town are depicted on this postcard from a century ago. The local gentry – surgeons, lawyers, bankers - lived or had business premises here at the east end of the Market Place from the middle of the 19th century. Some of these houses were demolished over 50 years ago and the land left derelict.

Below: This area today, with the open space tidied. That tidied space will be filled by a £2.5m welcome building to greet visitors to Auckland Castle. The building should open in spring 2016 (*left*).

5

This 1948 photograph shows the activity on a typical market day 70 years ago. Stalls packed on the restricted site in front of the town hall, and plenty of customers in attendance. Some of the old buildings on the north side, including the Angel Inn, King's Arms and Queen's Head are still in business.

Another packed market day scene c. 1937. This congestion was to remain until the mid 1980s. On the extreme right next to the Barrington School is Barclays Bank from which the previous photograph was taken.

That view in 2015 on a summer market Saturday. Hopefully the developments related to Auckland Castle will generate more business for the Market Place area.

The building housing Cherrett Bros., immediately to the left of the Queen's Head Hotel, was demolished in the 1950s, and the hotel car park opened there.

Queen's Head today, awaiting refurbishment along with next door the Kings Arms.

Duff & Rowntree on the south west corner of the Market Place, at the head of Newgate Street, c. 1930. The firm closed in 1936. Gills' House Furnishers had moved into the premises by 1937, but the facade of the building remained the same. By the 1970s Hintons supermarket was occupying a new building on the site (c. Beamish Museum).

Special Purchases for this Month
AT
DUFF & ROWNTREE'S,
THE POPULAR DRAPERS,
BISHOP AUCKLAND.

PLEASE NOTE:—
The Lot of Ladies' 4 Button Kid Gloves, that we are selling at 1/11½ per pair.
Specially Cheap Lots of Ladies' & Men's Hose, Bags, Umbrellas and Sunshades
Specially Cheap Lots of New Dress and Mantle Trimmings.
Specially Cheap Lots of New Blouses, Jerseys, and Ladies' Shirts.
Specially Cheap Lots of New Millinery Hats, Bonnets &c., of the Newest Designs
Specially Cheap Lots of New Skirts, Corsets, and Underclothing.
AT
Duff & Rowntree's.

A Duff & Rowntree advert from 'Hand Book of the World's Fair, Sale of Work and Wild West Entertainment' in Auckland Park from 14-17 June 1893.

The corner of the Market Place today. Not a very striking building compared to its predecessor though in terms of usage it has been transformed into an art gallery and studios providing local enterprises to gain a foothold in commerce and develop their businesses.

This is a more modern postcard than some of those seen so far, but it still dates from 55 years ago in 1960. Unusually this view of Newgate Street is from the north. It shows, particularly on the left, some of the long established businesses that many readers will remember – C. Watson, Doggarts, Deftys, Marks & Spencer. On the right is Timothy Whites & Taylors and T. Burdess. This card was sent from Shildon by auntie Ethel to Miss Richardson, Leeming near Northallerton in July and comments on the usual staples of holidays, visiting and the weather.

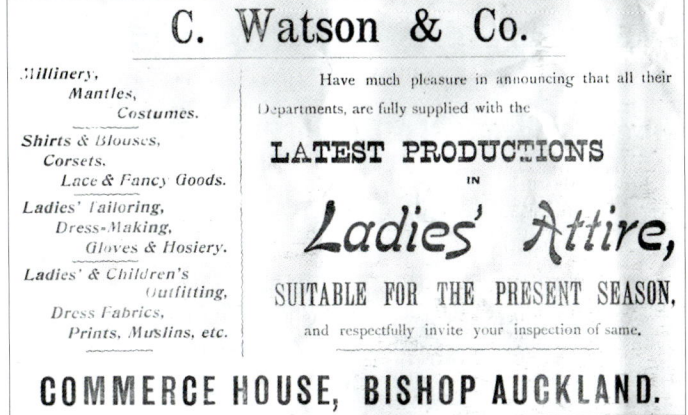

A Burdess advertisement from the 1948 town guide and one from C. Watson from much earlier 1902.

The top end of Newgate Street today, taken early one morning. However, the street is normally much less busy than in the above view, not helped by the empty shops and the gap on the left where the 'Mothercare' shop was demolished a few years ago because of safety concerns. The street is supposed to be pedestrianised, but the number of vehicles that travel down seems excessive.

Another card from the same publisher as the previous one – E. D. Walker & Wilson, Darlington – sent from Hettie in Bishop in August 1959 to Mr. W. E. Bateson, 14 Halton Place, Little Horton, Bradford saying "Dear Grandad & Winnie, having a nice time. Lovely weather. See you later." Short and sweet! Some well known shop fronts on the right – Maynards, Walter Willson, Charles Hall, and on the left - Hardys, Zip and Pickerings. At the head of Newgate Street the instantly recognizable 'Gill' sign. The street busy with a Rover 75 the leading vehicle travelling south.

Another photograph taken early one morning looking north up Newgate Street towards the Market Place. During the day, traffic – both moving and parked – makes it unrealistic to try and take such photographs. The old Walter Willson building is still there on the right, now occupied by Poundland.

A Gills' advertisement from the Coronation brochure of 1937, not long after they had taken over the old Duff & Rowntree building.

This postcard dates from c.1900 looking north from where Woolworth's was located in later years. The building at the head of Newgate Street has not yet been rebuilt by Duff & Rowntree and the new three storey building that opened as the King's Hall cinema in 1914 opposite the horse and cart has not appeared. The large building on the left is the Co-op. On the right is A. Cook newsagent which was taken over by W.H. Smith in the 1950s.

Right: A. Cook was long established in the town – this advertisement dates from the 1902 Coronation brochure of Edward VII. In the building housing the King's Hall cinema was also a lending library and restaurant as shown in this advertisement from 1937. In a 1921 carnival brochure it states that "the Kings Hall Orchestra plays daily in the tea-room."

A. COOK,
Bookseller,
Stationer and Newsagent,
49 Newgate Street,
Bishop Auckland.

KINGS LENDING LIBRARY

2D. PER VOLUME / WEEK   NO DEPOSIT

DAILY 9 a.m. to 8 p.m.

THE KINGS RESTAURANT & BALLROOM
NEWGATE STREET

Telephone 128.

The largest, most centrally situated Cafe Restaurant in town.

The manageress invites your catering
:: enquiries for Banquets, Dinners, ::
Wedding Receptions and Dances.

SMALL PRIVATE ROOMS AVAILABLE FOR HIRE.

Left: That scene in 2015 early on a Sunday morning, with many of the buildings having steel shutters protecting their windows and displays.

Right: This February 1927 programme shows films at the Kings Hall and Hippodrome, and the final week of the pantomime Cinderella at the Eden Theatre. The films in those days were silent, but later on in that year the first 'talkie', the Jazz Singer was released. It is reasonable to assume that all three venues in Bishop were showing 'talking' films when they were first released. Note no performances on a Sunday.

This 1960 photograph shows the Eden Theatre at the junction of Newgate Street and Princes Street, looking no different from 1892 when it was renamed, rebuilt and enlarged at a cost of £1,800 by Stan Laurel's father, Arthur Jefferson. Over the years the premises was a theatre, then cinema, then theatre and so on. In 1960 the films advertised were Tommy Steele in Tommy the Toreador and George Baker in The Moonraker. Newgate Street congested as usual (c. Beamish Museum).

The junction of Newgate Street with Princes Street and South Church Road is now very different from 50 years ago. The Eden Theatre was demolished in 1974 and the junction remodelled. On the extreme left is the statue of Stan Laurel

The Stan Laurel statue erected in 2008. This year 2015 was the 50th anniversary of his death in Hollywood, and 125 years after his birth in 1890.

A postcard sent in the early days of World War 1 on 26 November 1914 from Ellen in Bishop Auckland to Mrs Epps, 3 East Street, Faversham, Kent with the message "I was very pleased indeed to get your card, and thank you very much for kind thoughts and good wishes." The very modern Wesleyan church built in 1910 at a cost of £12,000 is front left. The entrance to Chester Street is on the right.

The Wesleyan Church is now the Four Clocks centre and used for social and leisure activities. This is an early morning shot before the build-up of two-way motor traffic. Chester Street is now one way. All the sun awnings have been removed.

The southern part of Newgate Street when it was known as South Road. The Wear Valley Hotel is on the right, then Samuel T. Light, and further away Brotherton who have been trading in the town since 1842. This postcard, with the posed figures in the foreground, dates from c. 1911. Charles Walker the proprietor of the hotel lived in the 27 roomed building with his wife, four adult children and seven servants at the 1911 census.

The Wear Valley Hotel 50 years later. The door canopy is missing, but otherwise remarkably unchanged. Note Brotherton's still two doors away, but with a modern facade. Much more traffic in this 1963 photograph.

The derelict Wear Valley Hotel in early 2002 in the process of demolition.

The scene today with Hewitts solicitors building replacing the Wear Valley Hotel in late 2002.

Rather ancient Newgate Street advertisements from 100 – 120 years ago. Some of these shops and firms still have a presence in Bishop Auckland today. The advertisements come from publications about royalty celebrations, church anniversary or fetes and official council publications. The dates are the years of publication.

This is one of the oldest advertisement for Walter Willson, grocer 1893.

Mrs Messenger, confectioner & caterer 1915.

M. Braithwaite & Son, stationer 1909.

Arthur Pulford, slater & tiler 1902.

W. Gregory, butcher 1911.

T. & G. O. Moses, watchmaker 1915.

Then & Now – Round the Town including South Church

Bondgate is the earliest identifiable street in the town running from the original village at Newton Cap eastwards towards the Bishop of Durham's castle. This postcard shows the Fleece Hotel (formerly the Golden Fleece) c. 1910. It was built on the site of a smithy early in the 19th century and had stabling facilities as indicated. Before the railway age both freight and passengers were carried by horse-drawn coach or cart all over the county. The landlord immediately before World War 1 was Edward Brighton Adams who hailed from Alnwick, Northumberland. Where does the 'Brighton' come from?

The Fleece Hotel c. 1950. No real changes to the building, though the light above the entrance seems to be disused. The North Eastern Breweries was actually part of the Vaux Co. of Sunderland (c. Beamish Museum).

Part of Bondgate today. A pale shadow of its former self in terms of commercial activity. When buses from Willington and Weardale terminated at High Bondgate there used to be significant pedestrian traffic along Bondgate into the Market Place and Newgate Street. Much of that has disappeared though there is an intention to increase car parking capacity in North Bondgate which may help increase the footfall.

Another photograph from the Beamish archives dated 1974. The Wheatsheaf and Bondgate Motors (formerly part of the Shepherd's Inn) on the right, and Howes fish & chips, Butterfield newsagent and Greggs butchers on the left. The Wheatsheaf was another of Bondgate's old inns, being listed in White's directory of 1827 when Thomas Thompson was the landlord (c. Beamish Museum).

Further west in Bondgate today. The building skyline hasn't really changed. Another public house has disappeared, with the Wheatsheaf now Lacey's club. Just beyond the flag of St. George is the footpath through to the Newgate Centre.

High Bondgate c. 1930. One of the earliest parts of the town dating from the 12th century linking Town Head and the castle. The photographer is standing by the roadside just above the railway tunnel on the Durham branch line. Not that a stranger would know that there was a tunnel there. On the right between the parked bus and the spreading tree is the police station. In the distance the spires of the town hall and St. Anne's Church. Between the buses is the street originally known as Far (or Fore) Bondgate and to the left beyond the walkers is Back (or North) Bondgate.

High Bondgate on a high summer's day in 2015. The small bus terminus is long gone and also the police station and Sun Inn beyond on the right.

Wesleyan Chapel, North Bondgate. An impressive building was built by the Wesleyans in 1842 on the site of a previous chapel dating from 1804. It was rebuilt and enlarged at a cost of £3,000 in 1866 and was big enough to seat 750 worshippers. A lecture hall and vestries were added in 1890 at a cost of £750. This postcard is about 110 years old. The taller building to the left was the offices of Trotter, Bruce & Loft, solicitors.

Nowadays, any evidence of the Wesleyan Chapel has gone. The solicitors are still next door, now called Smith Roddam.

North Bondgate garage in 1963 – the ground floor of the closed chapel was used as part of the garage facilities.

Durham Road c. 1930 not long after opening. Ferens Brothers flour mill complex mid right; behind are the houses of brothers Angus and Henry. The old way into Bishop from Durham is hidden between the railings and the mill building.

This Ferens advert for self-raising flour from the 1948 town guidebook helped signal the death-knell of the baking powder business of Bishop Auckland company Joseph Lingford.

Durham Road in the 1950s from the other direction. A wagon running on the old road from Castle and Gib chares coming up to the junction. Note the embankment lifting the main road up into the Market Place. Mill on the left.

A 2015 view of Durham Road looking towards the Market Place. The main visible change is the removal of the mill and building of houses. However, at the top the road now swings left towards Kingsway and vehicles must make a right turn into the Market Place

A postcard published within days of the War Memorial being unveiled on 13 September 1922. It was originally sited at the junction of the station approach with Newgate Street. At that date the inscription read "1914-1919. To the Men of Bishop Auckland who fought and fell in the Great War. Their fellow citizens have erected this Memorial." The site at the station approach was appropriate as the majority of men who went to the Great War would have left the town by train.

A photograph of the War Memorial now sited in the Market Place near St. Anne's Church. The memorial has no names inscribed upon it, but in the adjacent church is a wooden plaque with some names on it that individual families have sponsored. Over 1400 men who enlisted in Bishop Auckland died in World War One, but it is not known how many were from the town itself. Second World War figures show that over 2900 men who were killed in that war were born in County Durham.

King James I Grammar School boys of 1914 and 1939 who went to war and did not return. This plaque is located in King James Academy, South Church Road.

The 1857 railway viaduct from the 14th century road bridge. The houses are in Gomer Terrace on the left and the Batts through the arches on the right. The viaduct of 11 arches, 100 feet high served as a rail bridge until 1968.

Another early 20th century view of the viaduct, with the houses in Brancepeth Terrace in the shadow of the arches. Behind the trees is the incinerator and well.

The viaduct over 100 years later, now a road bridge with a concrete raft laid on the old track bed to allow widening of the carriageway. Brancepeth Terrace has disappeared.

The Roman Catholic Church in Bishop dating from 1846 and costing £1,000. In the language of the time Kelly's Directory 1914 describes it as having 500 sittings. Next to it was the local church school opened in 1874 and accommodating 400 children, infants and mixed. In front is the water fountain – for animals – which would have been heavily used by the residents of Town Head in the early years of the last century.

The scene today. The church is partly hidden by Bishopgate Lodge Care Home which is built on the old school site. St. Wilfrid's School is now located at Woodhouse Close. The water fountain remains as a monument separated by the wall and railings from the new housing behind.

'The Bridge on Wear, Bishop Auckland' is the caption on this card posted on 30 October 1913 from Mari at North Bondgate House, Bishop Auckland to Mr. John Hudson, 22 The Summit, Liscard, Cheshire. The message says "Here is a very good wish, indeed the best of wishes to you from an old pal. With love to Mrs Hudson. Trusting you are both well. I have been here a fortnight getting the house ready for Mrs F." A clearly defined photograph showing the two bridges, Newton Cap, Gomer Terrace on the far side of the river, and back left the pit heap of Newton Cap Colliery.

The 1913 view could not really be replicated today as the tree growth hides the bottom of Newton Cap bank. The viaduct provides the one point of similarity. In the far distance above the viaduct is a bungalow associated with Binchester Hall Farm, by the Roman fort.

In this view the photographer was positioned in about the same place as on the above old picture, but facing south west rather than north east. In the far distance is Escomb. Much nearer on this side of the River Wear are the roofs of the buildings at West Mill. This card was posted a year earlier on 8 September 1912 from Darlington to Miss B. Lee, 18 Mount St., Dorking, Surrey. The message is incomplete – "Dear B, "Arrived home safe. Nice journey, only two stops. Had to have a centre seat. Reached home at 3.30. Up again at 8. Pleased to say I found ..." This was the first of at least two cards sent! This view could not be replicated today because of housing development in Etherley Lane and vegetation growth.

Newton Cap Bank in this postcard c. 1920. The Bridge Hotel selling Cameron's ales is at the bottom, the Wesleyan Chapel on the right half-way up the bank, and the spire of St. Wilfrid's R.C. Church at the top. The cottages to the right of the bridge date from the 18th century. Behind the bushes on the left is the incinerator chimney. This postcard was sent on 25 April from Durham to Mrs. J. Clegg, 28 Springfield St., Eightlands, Dewsbury, Yorks and says "Dear Aunt, Uncle, All being well I will be coming home tomorrow night, but I hope you have had a nice holiday. The weather has been very bad. Had to stay in nearly all the time, but better today. We are going to Durham. With best love. Your loving niece, Edith." The British obsession with the weather!

Newton Cap bank in 2015. A number of the houses on the bank and in adjacent West Bridge Street and Lower Bridge Street have been demolished, along with the incinerator and the chapel. Bishopgate Lodge Care Home is the large building across the top of the photograph. Note the old fashioned lamp standard which appears on the 1920 postcard is still there in the centre of the bridge. The one on the far side has gone.

The Dam Head looking upstream, with the River Wear in full flow. The salmon boxes this side of the river allowed fish to migrate upstream and this was also the point where the weir diverted water north eastwards. The weir and sluice originally dated from the early 19th century and provided water for the corn mill and iron foundry and later the council water works.

The site of the Dam Head today with the dam and salmon boxes removed. The concrete debris is the limited evidence of its existence. The river flow much lighter in this summer shot.

Looking north east along the mill race at the Dam Head, c. 1915. This coloured postcard was sent from Maude at Allansford House, Cockton Hill, Bishop Auckland to Miss Phyllis Dixon, c/o Mrs Robinson, Cavendish House, Newcomen Terrace, Redcar.

Unfortunately, the stamp has been torn off, so we can't date it more accurately.

Above the Dam Head showing the weir and sluice gates, 1910. Boys swimming on a summer's day. An activity which continued well into the 1950s.

The same area today with no sign of the dam. This photograph was taken on a sunny afternoon in August – yet 50 years ago the site would have been crowded with children swimming, fishing and generally enjoying themselves!

Durham Chare a century ago with Ferens mill at the bottom adjacent to the River Gaunless. This road was one of the old ways into the town from Durham before Durham Road was built in the late 1920s. This postcard called 'Durham Chase' in error. A summer scene.

The same scene in the winter of 1910. The cold is obvious in this scene! The card, however, was posted in Bishop Auckland on 22 August 1913 from Phil to her uncle Mr. W. Lishman, Harewell House, Dacre Banks, near Leeds and amongst other things says "Have the 25 girls been yet … Has the pig got calves yet?" This card is one of a short series from a local photographer – another one in the series was posted from Coundon to Filey on 15 February 1910 and makes reference to the rough weather.

Durham Chare today. The building on the right and the wall providing the location connection with the two previous postcards.

Castle Chare – the old road into the Market Place from Durham. The gatehouse lodge of the castle is in the background. A Christmas postcard sent from Rita in Bishop on 29 December 1909 to Mrs Andrews, Hallgarth Lodge, Cotherstone, near Darlington with the following message: "Very many thanks for stamps for baby. Jack is going to buy him something in S and send it through. We had a very jolly Xmas here, Xmas tree and stockings hung up. Wishing you all a very happy New Year. With love, Rita." This picture was taken from behind the 'Temperance Society' drinking fountain.

It is impossible to replicate the scene today in that the embankment supporting Durham Road in the background hides any buildings, i.e. castle and adjacent houses. In addition Castle Chare at the top is bisected by the comparatively new road swinging round into Kingsway. Consequently, the Chare is rarely used, overgrown and litter-strewn.

The Temperance Society drinking fountain dating from 1873. Still there but usually hemmed in by parked cars.

South Lane, 1907. A card posted in Bishop on 3 January from S. Stubbs to Miss Jane Pearson, Hinderwell S. O. wishing her a Happy New Year. King James 1 Grammar School 1864 building on the right, opposite the Trinity Presbyterian Church of England building dating from 1863. South Lane was renamed South Church Road only a few years after.

King James 1 Grammar School, c. 1905 – 300 years after the founding of the school in 1605. The building was extended after 1873 to accommodate 150 boys plus a handful of boarders. Stan Laurel was a boarder in 1902 after his family had moved from Bishop to North Shields. In my time at the school from 1954 the building was used for art, physics, chemistry and as VI forms common rooms.

The building after being ravaged by fire in 2007. It was 'made safe' immediately afterwards and has remained in this condition since, gradually deteriorating as time passes.

The building in July 2015 eight years after the arson attack. The old view on this page cannot be replicated as trees now mask the building. There is a proposal to renovate the building and use it as a small business start-up centre, but that is dependent upon funds being secured.

Recreation Ground in 1943 showing the bowling green and in the background the bandstand. A postcard from Margaret in Bishop to her parents Mr. & Mrs J.J. Lister, 1 Market Street, Blackhill – "having a grand time, but not very nice weather. Got your letters alright. Will be home sometime Monday."

The bowling green today. The bandstand has now gone. Out of shot is a club house and tennis courts.

Lady Eden Cottage Hospital, Cockton Hill with the matron Miss E. Burnett standing outside in 1936. To her left is the foundation stone dating from 23 July 1898. Before the National Health Service was set up in 1948, this hospital and the one on the opposite side of Cockton Hill Road which was part of Bishop Auckland Poor Law Institution (workhouse) were the main medical establishments, apart from general practitioners, in the

town. The hospital formally opened on 8 September 1898 as a consequence of the efforts of Lady Sybil Eden (Anthony Eden's mother) and others connected with the

Church and coal mining industry. In the early days it played a significant role in the treatment of men injured in the coal mines and other industrial concerns in the area (c. Beamish Museum).

Left: A postcard published by the Auckland Times & Herald commemorating the formal opening of the hospital in 1899.

Eden House is a 53 bed care home completed in October 2013 and built on the site of the hospital which had closed 2006/7. The modern photograph shows how the west front facade of the 1898 building has been retained with a two storey redevelopment behind. Note the original foundation stone still in place.

Cockton Hill Road on a postcard sent from Bishop Auckland to Mrs J. Kidd, 27 Station Road, Norton-on-Tees in October 1916 from Reyhill (?), Northumberland Avenue. The card has about 20 lines of closely spaced writing on it – neat, but very difficult to read. On the right is the Primitive Methodist Church built 1903 and on the left the Baptist Church dating from 1911.

A modern view of Cockton Hill Road. Both churches are still in use, though the Baptist Church is hidden by the trees. The building in the distance on the right-hand side of the road is the Green Tree Hotel. Normally the traffic on this road is heavy, so taking a photograph in the road itself could be dangerous.

Right: This postcard was probably printed by local publisher G.W.R. (Rudd) not long after the P.M. Church opened as it was posted on 10 October 1905 by E.R. in Bishop to Miss M. Relton, 100 Parliament Street, Middlesbrough. The writer says "T.E.R. is coming to the Primitive affair" – maybe a reference to the picture on the front.

Far right: The Methodist Church today – the main one in the town of that denomination. The church seems to have lost some frontage as Acacia Road was built between it and Lady Eden Cottage Hospital sometime around 1906-09. In the 1911 census there was only one house in Acacia Road.

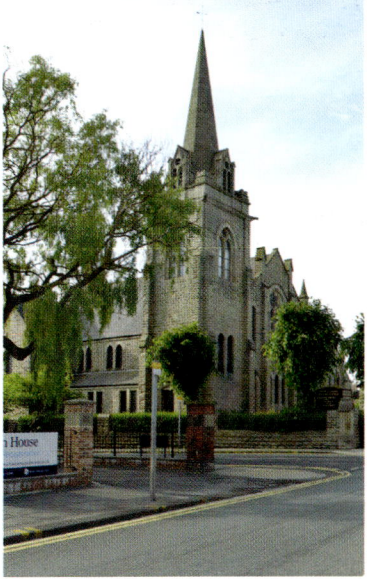

Cabin Gate, Bishop Auckland in 1934. Ossie Huntly's Motor Supplies on the right at the junction with St. Andrew's Road; on the left the Woodhouse Lane junction. He sold Chevrolet cars – that company had been founded in 1911 in Detroit, United States (c. Beamish Museum).

Cabin Gate 80 years on. Another location which always seems busy with motor vehicles. There's been some tree trimming to the left and the ivy has been removed from the building near left.

Right: Brack or Brack's Wood, c. 1908. Note the well-kept path and fencing guarding the stream, and the two men posed for the camera. This postcard was sent from B.R. in Bishop Auckland on 8 February 1908 to Miss E. Hind, St. Hild's College, Durham with the following message: "How would a walk suit here? Coming through to see you some time soon. Best love. C.Y.K. 10 times." I assume C.Y.K. is an affectionate greeting!

Far right: Brack's Wood in early spring 2015. The stream which flows into the River Gaunless about 100 yards away on the right is still there, but no fencing. The path doesn't seem very well used apart from dog walkers.

The metal bridge over the River Gaunless connecting the original nine acre part of the town cemetery to the new part. There was a bridge here in 1896 twelve years after the cemetery opened leading into Brack's Wood, though this bridge dates from 1909 when presumably the cemetery extension was mooted.

That bridge today with the scene largely unchanged though the gate at the far end has been removed. There is still significant traffic over this bridge with hearses, mourners cars and council vehicles.

A tranquil scene about 110 years ago on the River Gaunless. The man in the straw boater is sitting opposite the sluice gates entrance to the mill race where water was diverted into Ferens mill about 600 yards down river. There's a weir a few yards downstream from where he's sitting.

Above: Vegetation has very much reclaimed this area today and this was in early March. The sluice has gone along with the mill race which has been filled in. Further upstream is a modern pedestrian bridge over the Gaunless.

Left: The overgrown and tumbledown entrance to the mill race today.

The chapel in the town's cemetery is shown on this postcard sent from Barnard Castle on 30 June 1909. The writing on the reverse from Fred to his aunt Mrs Huggin, 1 Valley Road, Littlemoor, Pudsey, Leeds is very clear – "Bertha finds she can manage the journey on Thursday. She will write to you soon after she reaches Devonport. Love from all." Whellan's 1893 directory says of the cemetery: 'The Bishop Auckland and District Cemetery, opened in 1884, is very pleasantly situated on the Gaunless, a little south-east of the town, on the road to South Church. It comprises an area of ten acres, about a third of which is understood to be set aside for Catholics. There is a neat mortuary chapel in the early English style, also a good house for the superintendent.'

This memorial on the right is to Robert Watson who died on 9 May 1891. However, there are some interesting features to the structure: it is made of metal and 'pings' if you tap on it.

A close-up of the memorial. We'll return to Mr Watson on page 60.

Jock's Bridge in c. 1910 at the junction of the rivers Wear and Gaunless. The two/three roomed cottages behind were called Jock's Row, with nine households listed in the 1911 census. All the nine householders bar one (a widow) were coal hewers. Town hall is on the skyline back right.

Left: The proposal to tender for the building of a new Jock's Row bridge 1819. There had been a bridge here in the 18th century, but it was probably damaged in the great flood of 1771 when the River Wear changed its course and many of the houses in Jock's Row were swept away.

Below: Today's photograph shows the date 1819 on the right (upstream) keystone. Some of the coping stones on the bridge parapet have been replaced over the years.

Left: Wear Chare, c. 1908 with the children in front of the well and the railings in front of the late 18th century houses.

Below: Looking up Wear Chare in about 1860. Note the houses were lower than the road. Some of those railings survived until the 1950s.

Above: In 2008 Northumbrian Water were working in Wear Chare and in their excavations came across the flagstone floors of one of the 18th century cottages – possibly no. 34 whose disused cellar was used as an air-raid shelter in the Second World War. By 2008 the houses had been demolished nearly seven decades.

Left: This photograph from 2008 had to be taken in the spring as in high summer the bottom of the bank is hidden by foliage. The houses next to the former public house bottom left were demolished c. 1960 leaving the early 20th century three houses on the right, plus the converted pub and little cottage attached to it. Water from the site of the old well still seeps on to the path.

St. Andrew's Church, South Church on a postcard from a century ago which looks as though it was taken from St. Andrew's Road. The largest parish church in the county, St. Andrew's has a length of 157 feet and transept width of 80 feet and dates from the 13th century.

The church today, partly hidden by the tree cover. Men working on the roof to the right in this early October 2015 picture.

South Church   Bishop Auckland

Above: The church in 1901, taken from the road to West Deanery. Note the closeness of the River Gaunless to the houses, particularly those on the right in Pease, Middle and Perkins streets. This colour printed card has probably been 'touched up' by the publisher.

Below: The view a century later. The flood prevention work south of Spring Gardens, West Auckland after the floods of 2000 hopefully will prevent any repetition of the distress caused 15 years ago in South Church.

An 1852 sketch of St. Andrew's Church.

South Church   Bishop Auckland

Main Street in 1966; two houses already empty next to the Primitive Methodist Chapel. The old brewery building on the right dominated the street.

That view in early summer 2015. A better view of the church, though the poles, bus stop and trees detract somewhat.

By 1967 most of Victorian South Church in terms of housing had disappeared. This photograph taken from near the River Gaunless shows the open spaces created by demolition a few years earlier (c. Beamish Museum).

That scene today with new housing screening the church somewhat. The one constant is St. Andrew's Church.

INTERESTING ITEMS INCLUDING GONE BUT NOT FORGOTTEN

There are a number of places and features in Bishop Auckland that have disappeared either through demolition, re-development or they just fell down. The following pictures may remind the reader of times past when, maybe as children, they were familiar with places like the wishing temple or the doctor's tunnel to name just a couple. Also, there are features of interest still around that very few people knew about in the first place!

We'll start in the Bishop's park at a location where there was a bridge across the River Gaunless, but not the one that any reader will be familiar with. About 200 yards north of the deer house was a footbridge which appears on the 1857 Ordnance Survey map of the town. By 1896 the footbridge was no more. The temple and broad walk footbridge also appear.

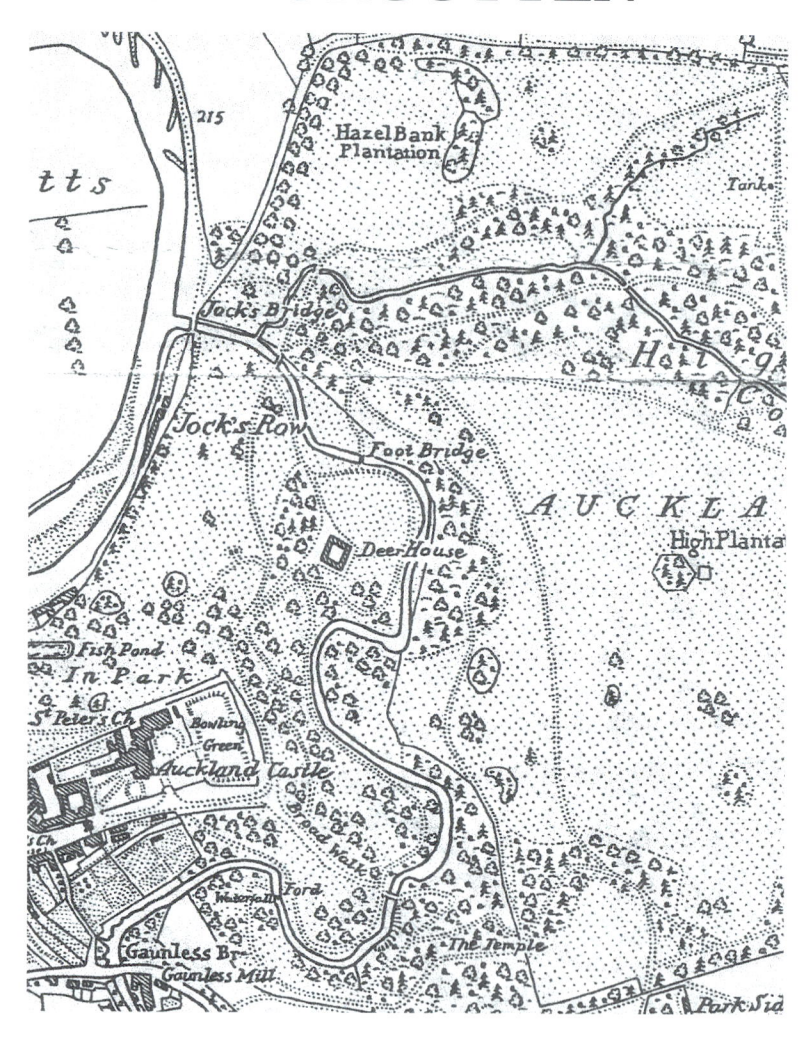

The site of that bridge today. There are some stones supporting the river bank on the south side, but without the 1857 map, the location is very difficult to find. However, the bridge leads to "two trees, planted on the island opposite the Barrington oak" as quoted by Matthew Richley in his 1872 History and Characteristics of Bishop Auckland. The inscriptions on stones near these two trees are as follows: "This oak, then 18 feet high, was planted by Bishop Maltby, November 5th, 1841" and "This oak, then 14 feet high, was planted by the Rev. H.J. Maltby, youngest son and chaplain to the Bishop of Durham, November 5th 1841."

44

The stones today. This land is low-lying and possibly boggy in winter, but is not an island, and is well covered with trees. However, 170 years ago the terrain could have been wetter and the River Gaunless wilder. The two oaks are very tall, but do compete with other trees and shrubs for the available space. The Barrington oak mentioned above was planted in 1794 a short distance south of the 1757 drive bridge.

The oak today next to the stone commemorating the planting of it by Bishop Maltby. The other oak is a few yards further on towards the left.

The Bishop – as a man of substance – had an ice-house- just to the north of the drive bridge in the park. It was set in the hillside and provided ice to the castle kitchens in the summer. This ice-house, now bricked up, is about half-a-mile north of the castle. Why such a long way from the castle? It is located on the old carriage road to Durham via Park Head

The more well known footbridge in the park at the end of the broad walk and leading to the wishing temple also appears on the 1857 map and lasted to the middle of the 20th century. This card was sent from Joe in Willington in 1912 to Mrs Oliphant, Cross House Farm, Allendale, Northumberland and says: "Yours to hand. I have had a nice letter from Gilsland. All is keeping very quiet here although there are a lot starving. I wish the strike was settled; it is affecting everybody. No word from Glaister yet. What about Gloves and what about trains. Love to all." There was a miners strike in 1912 which is presumably what he is referring to. The bridge was still in use in the 1950s, but does not appear on a 1962 map.

Another view from downstream of the bridge on this card. Note the centre bridge support which appears on cards published after World War One. This card was sent from Cis and Arthur and sent to Miss King, 37 Belfast Street, Hove Sussex. The message talks about visiting the park and castle.

Above and right: The site of the bridge today. The bridge supports and steps are still visible and also the concrete 'pad' in the middle of the river. There was a proposal by Bishop Auckland Lions to have the bridge rebuilt in the early 1990s, but that came to nought.

WISHING TEMPLE, BISHOP AUCKLAND PARK. (7)

The wishing temple dates from 1810 and is identified as 'The Temple' on the 1857 map. A number of my postcards of the temple which show the adjacent trees had initials carved on them 100 years ago. Was the temple a venue for young lovers in those far off days?

Above: It is very difficult to identify the site of the temple today as it was pulled down in 1961. There are some stones hidden in the undergrowth, but the means of identifying the exact site was a combination of map reading and the location of the trees.

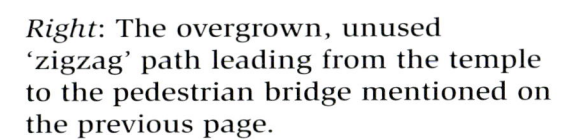

Right: The overgrown, unused 'zigzag' path leading from the temple to the pedestrian bridge mentioned on the previous page.

This postcard probably dates from 1912 when as a consequence of a mining dispute, striking miners dug for coal on the High Plains where the coal seam outcropped above the River Gaunless. The Bishop is said to have turned a blind eye to the practice which happened again a few times during the General Strike of 1926 and the Depression years which followed. The figures may well be men from Jock's Row and Dial Stob Hill which dwellings were only a few minutes walk from the outcrop – they would climb over the park wall which skirted the houses.

This photograph of mine from 1988 is in the area of the coal mining on the previous photograph. The coal mining itself probably undermined the cliff face over a long period.

A major landslip about 14 years later took away much of the cliff face and the scree below it, so it is far more difficult today to determine where that mining occurred. Certainly it was north east of the deer house on the east bank of the river, but the changes in topography and vegetation growth 100 years on leave a margin for error in terms of the exact location. This photograph was taken in March 2015 before trees and bushes were in full bloom.

48

The effects of pollution from flooded old mine workings can still be seen. This photograph upstream from the previous three shows tainted water flowing into the River Gaunless.

The drive bridge in the park was built by order of Bishop Trevor and has his initials – RD (Richard Dunelm) and the building date of 1757 on the left (downstream) keystone. This is a very substantial structure as can be seen from the bottom two photographs, though the actual width of the carriageway seems rather narrow. I could not identify the Barrington oak which Richley in 1872 says lies south of the drive bridge.

Early in 2015 there was significant newspaper correspondence about the 'Doctors Tunnel' at the rear of Bondgate in Bishop Auckland.
It is thought that extensions to the rear of the former Shepherd's Inn in the early 19th century had impinged upon a well-established footpath that resulted in the building of a tunnel under the extension thus allowing the public to still use the right of way from Newgate Street via William Street to Fenkle Street and Hamburgh Square (1857 map). The inn was later split in two into 'Ye Old Oakland Inn' and Zairs cafe. The tunnel was filled with concrete in June 1981 when the area was being cleared in preparation for the building of the Newgate Centre. The footpath by then had also gone as part of the redevelopment. Fortunately, the photograph shown was taken in the early 1970s and shows the ten or so steps down into the tunnel which stretched for about 15 yards and had a similar number of steps up at the other end. Note the map shows it has a bridge (over the path) and the name 'Doctors' is said to derive from a Dr. Martin Dunn who owned this large house in Bondgate before it became an inn, and he held consultations in the room over the path.

The steps at the western end of the tunnel were located where this concrete mass is today. The building shown in the photograph above has been cut back as part of the developments associated with the Newgate Centre. The other photograph is of the front of the building today accommodating Sam Zair's cafe and the Spice Lounge. The upstairs window surrounds betray the building's 19th century origins.

The Odeon cinema just before and a while after closure. By which time the large vertical 'Odeon' sign had disappeared from above the canopied entrance. It was by far the most comfortable cinema in the town and had started off life as the 'Majestic' – by which name in the 1950s many older residents still called it.

A rare photograph of the Odeon taken by the owners. Some facts: opened 21 November 1938 as the Majestic; 1380 seats. Taken over by the Odeon Cinemas organization 12 March 1944 and renamed on 2 April 1945. Converted into a twin cinema 13 May 1973, with 552 and 123 seats respectively. Closed 15 October 1983.

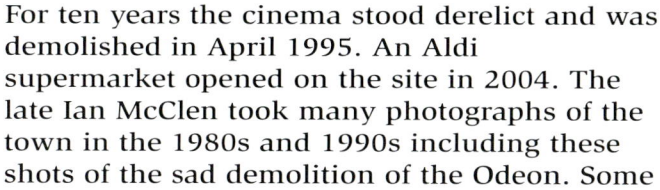

For ten years the cinema stood derelict and was demolished in April 1995. An Aldi supermarket opened on the site in 2004. The late Ian McClen took many photographs of the town in the 1980s and 1990s including these shots of the sad demolition of the Odeon. Some readers may be able to remember the inside of the building as they knew it in their Saturday children's matinee or courting days in the double seats!

The Sun Inn, next to the police station, is where Mary Ann Cotton had her meals when she appeared at Bishop Auckland committal hearings on murder charges between August 1872 and February 1873. Its other main claim to fame is that it was taken down brick by brick and re-erected in the main street of the town at Beamish Open Air Museum. The first photograph is the inn in its original state in High Bondgate, Bishop Auckland next to the police station 1964.

The next photograph is of the inn closed up; the police station already demolished.

Dismantling of the inn as the first stage of its transport to Beamish in 1982 (c. Beamish Museum).

The Sun Inn, Beamish 2015. I don't think there is any reference to its most infamous visitor at the inn today, but you can still get a pint. It is small with just a bar and a rather dark snug.

An inscription on the western parapet of the 14th century road bridge over the River Wear at Newton Cap commemorates Edwd. Palfrey, a renowned prizefighter, who in a drunken state after a fight against a bull had been cancelled, fell off the bridge parapet whilst 'entertaining' the crowd. He eventually leaped off twice more, but on that third jump the inevitable happened – he 'dashed his brains out.' This was in 1744 as the inscription says. This first photograph was taken by Keith Cockerill in 2004, but the inscription is still as fresh today (second photo) on the top of the stone parapet on the upstream (west) side of the northern (Toronto)arch at approximately the mid point of the arch. The stone is slightly larger than the ones on either side as it sticks out a couple of inches over the river below. The other interesting point of note is that the inscription is carved upside down. The first photograph in the book has been turned through 180 degrees whereas the second is as taken.

In December 2013 there was an arson attack on the former St. Anne's School building in Kingsway, Bishop Auckland. The school had closed to pupils over 40 years earlier in 1971 and until recent years had been used as education offices by the county council. Later part of it was used as a church community hall. However, it had been closed for a number of years and inevitably had started to deteriorate and suffer from break-ins. The school buildings are now a sad sight as shown in these photographs from September 2015, so before it is too late a short resume on the school and its history, particularly as I was a pupil there from 1948 to 1954, is appropriate.

St. Anne's C. of E. School 1951, class 5. Back left: Peter Haddon, John Ogilvy, Billy Mounsey, Colin Gregg, Harry Coglan, Gordon Rutherford, Chris Dunn, Harold Briggs, Freddy Clayton. Middle left: Stuart Robinson, Tommy Hutchinson, David Leighton, Josephine Weatherburn, Barbara Brown, Albert Hawkes, Gerald Tipling, Alan Hall, Terry Barker. Front left: Eileen Coglan, Loretta Norton, Treffie Nodding, Joan Stocks, Eileen Fitzgerald, Avril Withers, Marion Soulsby, Mary Gibbon, Anne Briddick, Pauline Mudd.

The following notes are based on a book written by F. M. Carr in 1972 when school log books were used to give a picture of life at the school over a century.

The school opened in 1833 supported by the Church of England on land east of the almshouses in Bishop Auckland Market Place as a "school of industry" for girls and infants to complement Barrington Boys' School in the Market Place. In 1856 the governors set up a separate new girls and infants schools in Kingsway for "children of the labouring, manufacturing and other poorer classes in the parish of St. Andrew's." The school then continued as two separate entities for 100 years. In 1898 a new wing was built and the 1856 building extensively altered. In 1930 the girls' school became a junior mixed and in 1957 the infant school was amalgamated with it. The school closed in summer 1971 when the new St. Anne's School opened in Warwick Road, Bishop Auckland.

The following log entries hopefully give a flavour of the school. Before 1930 the entries are for the girls' school only.

12 May 1863 – 23 girls kept in at noon to write the word 'late' for being late.

16 September 1863 – several ask leave of absence on account of 'Mothers washing day.'

8 July 1864 – leave given to M. Kavanaugh to come in at 10 a.m. every morning while employed in the hayfield.

19 January 1865 – a great many children in Section 111 sent home for slates … through neglect of parents to provide them with such articles …

21 February 1866 – I … Perryman has an infectious eruption on her and will probably be absent some time.

2 September 1869 – Auckland Flower Show – a holiday.

14 September 1871 – Visited several absentees. C. Wilkinson has smallpox, Grace and Elizabeth Gregory's uncle has typhoid fever and Sarah Symons sister has just died of the same.

4 August 1874 – Three girls named Chapman have been withdrawn … because their father objects to their curtseying on leaving the room. This is an old rule and cannot be departed from.

27 September 1875 – very poor attendance … owing to the Railway Jubilee held at Darlington.

12 November 1878 – terrific snowstorm: very few children came to school.

17 January 1881 – about 100 present. Weather frightfully cold. No copy writing could be taken. Ink in the wells frozen.

1 March 1883 – had to reprove Bel Breken for reading a book of an immoral kind.

20 February 1890 – examined Standard III. Reading good. Writing good. Arithmetic almost a total failure …

23 September 1893 – Mary Simpson … has died from diphtheria. There are a few cases of typhoid fever.

17 January 1898 – extension of the school buildings caused an additional weeks holiday. School re-opened this morning.

22 & 23 January 1901 – death of our beloved Queen. Short address to the school on the sad event after prayers.

12 June 1902 – average attendance 419.

1 April 1904 – school falls under authority of Durham County Council. No further school fees.

2 October 1907 – measles spreading; 3 October schools must be closed at noon today by order of Medical Authority … until 4 November.

31 January 1910 – streets almost impassable (snowstorm). Attendance poor.

5 October 1910 – half holiday. Opening of Girls' County School (later became grammar school).

18 September 1914 – poor attendance … throughout week. Recruiting for war and departure of relatives to various military depots has affected attendance considerably.

14 November 1917 – attendance this week has been greatly affected by parents sending children to stand in queues for butter etc.

13 November 1918 – Education Committee has granted holiday for the remainder of the week to celebrate the signing of the armistice.

24 September 1919 – school closed (Town's welcome to His Majesty's Forces).

6 June 1920 – to encourage saving of small sums the 'Yorkshire Penny Bank' system introduced.

27 September 1920 – Millicent Dobson has been presented with a framed certificate for never having been absent or late for six years ending 31 March 1920.

25 June 1926 – free meals for school children are being provided at the Edgar Hall.

30 June 1927 – school closed yesterday on account of solar eclipse … party of 100 girls … viewing the eclipse from Brusselton under supervision of the teachers.

1 February 1929 – 55 names have been sent to District Clerk for inclusion on School Feeding List.

24 June 1930 – it is proposed to re-organise this school as from August 1st next when it will become a Junior Mixed Department … probable number on roll will be 372. 8 September junior boys from the Barrington enrolled today.

21 March 1931 – official name of the school … Bishop Auckland St. Anne's C. of E. School No. 26.

25 August 1931 – Miss Jane Metcalfe took up duty as a Certified Assistant … her first appointment.

6 December 1934 – headmistress left school … in order to attend Social Service Centre during the visit of His Royal Highness the Prince of Wales.

31 January 1936 – the children were taken to market place to hear the Proclamation of the King.

4 October 1938 – distribution of gas masks has been completed …

1 August 1939 – children were assembled, given milk and then sent home because of the evacuation orders.

28 June 1940 – poor attendance this week because of several air raid warnings.

19 June 1942 – part of the railings have been removed for the war effort.

8 May 1945 – V.E. Day. Children assembled for a short service at 9 a.m.

27 March 1946 – school solid meals began today … 130 received meals.

5 September 1949 – the school house was inspected with view to making it into a staff room.

15 February 1952 – children observed two minutes silence … funeral of George VI.

22 May 1953 – Coronation Mugs were given to children. 2 June – Coronation Day being wet, children came to school instead of having sports, were given two bags of cakes, two bottles of mineral water, and an ice-cream each.

3 May 1955 – electricians came to install electricity.

29 October 1956 – central heating completed.

26 July 1957 – when the school re-opens the Infant and Junior Departments will be amalgamated under the headship of Mr. Sanderson. Miss Gray will retire from headship tonight.

12 July 1961 – pigeons have again found their way into the roof.

5 November 1962 – workmen commenced on room for partially deaf children.

6 November 1962 – partially deaf children started.

My Coronation mug, with the town's coat of arms on the other side. We were also given a propelling pencil, but that's long gone.

21 September 1964 – Mr. Sanderson … to retire 30 December.

28 January 1965 – Mr. Johnson appointed Head Teacher … from 26 April.

22 December 1967 – Mrs l. B. Atkinson retired after 21 years … Her successor Miss J. Metcalfe.

13 May 1971 – Miss J. Metcalfe to retire at end of term. 22 May – Mrs O.W. Swan appointed Deputy Head as from 31.8.71.

16 July 1971 – Miss Metcalfe retires after having taught 40 years at the school. After the holidays the School will remove to new premises in Warwick Road.

Pigot's directory of 1834 lists over 20 of taverns and public houses in Bishop Auckland, most of them in the Market Place, Bondgate and Newgate Street. Some of the names will be familiar such as the Angel, Bay Horse, Dun Cow, King's Arms, Three Tuns (two of them) and Wheatsheaf. Others not so familiar – Black Horse, Coach & Horses, Hare & Hounds, Malt Shovel, Tiger and William IV. There was also a brewer called Thomas Mills in Newgate Street and one inn & posting house – the Talbot in the Market Place. The Talbot was a stop for the coaches to and from Newcastle, Manchester and Liverpool, whilst most local carriers within the county and to Westmorland went from the Malt Shovel in Newgate Street. The rapid development of the town from the middle of the 19th century also resulted in new pubs opening, so that by the 1890s there were over 50 inns, hotels, taverns and beerhouses in the town, with one brewer – Bentley & Co. in Newgate Street. Over the years many of the pubs changed their names, presumably to more fashionable ones such as the Sun Inn from the Tiger, Commercial Hotel from the Hare & Hounds, or the Castle Hotel which started life as the Railway Hotel in the Market Place.

The regular visit to the public house remained a key leisure activity until after World War Two, but a notable feature after that war was the replacement by other commercial premises of pubs at the north end of Newgate Street. Perhaps there was more income available from selling commercial space to retail organisations other than for public houses in the 1950s. The top end of Newgate Street housed large retailers such as Boots, Doggarts, Co-operative Society, Marks & Spencer and Woolworths. Eventually, there was only one pub in Newgate Street north of the Eden Theatre and that was the redeveloped Silver Bugle (former Old Black Boy) instead of the twelve earlier in the century.

In 1963 a number of photographs were taken of many of the public houses left in Bishop Auckland. Since then more of them have disappeared. I attach a selection of those pubs which are no more and one or two that are still there.

Edinburgh Castle Inn on the north side of Bondgate photographed c. 1963. The inn opened c. 1860 and may have been originally a private house. It was small, only six rooms in total, including living accommodation. The pub is now a shop.

The Three Tuns in Bondgate – not to be confused with its namesake in Newgate Street. One of the older pubs in the town as it appeared in Pigot's directory. It was pulled down to make way for a pedestrian way from the 1980s Newgate Centre into Fore Bondgate. In a few yards on the right there was the Wheatsheaf, Shepherd's Inn (later Oakland Hotel), Three Tuns, Spirit Vaults and Golden Fleece up to the post war years.

Maid of Erin at 10 West Road was located opposite St. Wilfrid's Roman Catholic Church. It started life as a beerhouse in the late 19th century, possibly converted from a private house. At the 1911 census William and Mary Ann Peat were the innkeepers and they and their eight children lived in five rooms. His main occupation was as a coke drawer – maybe at nearby Newton Cap Colliery. It has reverted to the status of private house today.

Thompson Street was built in the late 1850s and appears on the 1857 Ordnance Survey map backing on to the newly opened railway line to Durham. The Harp Inn at no.9 seems to have been built as commercial premises from the outset, having a total of eight rooms in the building. At the 1861 census there was a total of twelve persons at the address, with two heads of households, one of them a beerhouse keeper by occupation. At the 1901 census the inn was identified as the Harp of Erin. In the 1970s the local council published a plan which proposed new roads, new bus station and Newgate Shopping Centre in the whole area between the shops on the west side of Newgate Street and the line of the now closed railway line. The Harp Inn was demolished along with the rest of Thompson Street plus Saddler, Grainger, George, Clayton, William, Wood streets, and Hall Terrace. The top end of Tenters Street also went. The DHSS building – a blot on the landscape – took their place as well as the developments mentioned above.

The Three Tuns Hotel in Newgate Street has completely disappeared, being replaced by a modern building occupied by Boots since 1976.

Right: Dick Brown and his father Richard and son, also called Richard, outside the Market Hotel, Newgate Street in the 1920s. The hotel, formerly called the Spirit Vaults (one of three in Bishop Auckland) dated from the middle of the 19th century. Only a small hotel with a total of eight rooms.

Far right: The site of the Market Hotel today. Now a Greggs shop. The first floor large window has been altered, with the bow and balcony above removed and decorative railings taken down.

Some pubs have survived in a different form. Newton Cap Hotel at the top of Newton Cap bank in this 1963 photograph (*above left*) is now Buddies childcare centre in this 2015 photograph (*above right*).

The occasional public house outside of the central area of the town has survived. The Welcome Inn in Lower Waldron Street appears in this photograph (*above left*) from over 60 years ago and is still thriving in 2015. The inn is on the site of Pollards Grange which appears as a country estate on the 1857 Ordnance Survey Map. In 1911 the inn of seven rooms was in the charge of Charles Robinson who was also a fruiterer. In the background is the railway line to Durham (c. Beamish Museum). 2015 saw the inn basking in the summer sunlight (*above right*).

At the entrance to the town's cemetery is a very large monument to Robert Watson who was buried there 12 May 1891. The monument – which is not concrete or stone in construction, but metal – was made in 1890 by the Monumental Bronze Company, Bridgeport, Connecticut, U.S.A. The Northern Echo of 11 and 13 May 1891 explains under a heading 'From Farm Servant to Mayor - The Story of a Self-made Man.' Robert as a youth was a farm servant at Hamsterley and Over Dinsdale. Then he worked as a railway platelayer between Leeds and Thirsk; an overseer on the Stockton & Darlington Railway and later in the Midlands. He went to America and became an inspector on the Alton & Illinois Railway. However, his ambitions were much higher and he went into land purchase, buying up lots, putting them into 'best condition' and selling at opportune moments. Sheep farming became another interest and at one time had as many as 3,000 in Kansas. He eventually was described as a nurseryman and dispatched fruit all over the U.S.A. as well having on hand 100,000 hedge plants. Robert, a bachelor, became involved in civic life and was a town councillor and subsequently mayor of Leo's Summit, Kansas and also tax surveyor at Springfield, Illinois. He retired in about 1884 and spent time travelling. Eventually, he came back to England and resided with his cousin Elizabeth Taylor and her husband Richard in Victoria Street, Bishop Auckland. The memorial and grave space in the cemetery was completed in 1890. He used to sit on one of the metal seats he had provided by the memorial and listen to the comments of the curious as they passed. There was some apparent criticism of him erecting his own monument, but he abided by a ruling principle to do everything decently and to be prepared for all eventualities. He made handsome benefactions to the inmates of Weardale and Auckland workhouses, gave to the poor of Auckland, Hamsterley and Wolsingham the previous Christmas, and also gave to other charitable organisations where he was remembered with respect and gratitude.

His grave is a little to the north west of the monument. Under the monument is a copy of the Northern Echo giving a description of the memorial and a sketch of the deceased gentleman in a sealed bottle. Also buried in that plot are Richard and Elizabeth Taylor who died in 1908 and 1909 respectively. The metal seats referred to above were removed many years ago.

The inscription on the front says 'To the memory of Robert Watson born at Hamsterley January 8, 1819, died at Bishop Auckland May 9, 1891.' Other inscriptions on the monument say 'With charity to all. An honest man is the noblest work of God. God has revealed himself in nature of which science is the interpreter. Be honest to thy God, the world, thy country, thy fellowmen and thyself.'

The gravestone for the Taylors has been pushed over. I think Robert Watson is buried at the foot of the cypress tree in the middle of the picture. The cypress is a tree native to North America – co-incidence?

In 1948 the Ministry of Education published a Local Studies pamphlet and film of eight studies by secondary school pupils on Bishop Auckland, covering research and visits to Wilson's Forge, Grange Hill and Binchester Hall farms. The 31 children were drawn from the two grammar schools, Cockton Hill, Barrington and St. Wilfrid's schools and would be in their 80s now. One group went to Binchester Hall Farm and the old photograph on the right shows their visit to the Roman fort. They are going down through the trap-door to see the hypocaust. Two of the children visiting Binchester were Ruth Jacques from Barrington and Ronald Hunter from Cockton Hill.

Nearly 60 years on a visit to Binchester does not involve trap-doors, crouching and darkness. The photograph above is of part of the hypocaust today, very accessible and housed in a weather-proof building.

Here are some of the recent excavations at Binchester which over the past years has revealed a lot more of the scale and size of the Roman fort and town (vicus) as well as many more finds dating from more than 1600 years ago. The photograph above is of trench one showing part of the cavalry barracks.

Right: This photograph of trench two shows part of a bath building first excavated in 2014 and further excavated this year.

RAILWAYS IN BISHOP AUCKLAND

From the 1960s the railway scene in the town changed enormously with passenger services to Durham, Barnard Castle and Crook ceasing, leaving only the service to Darlington. This was the culmination of a process of rationalization that had started as early as 1939 when the passenger service to Spennymoor ceased, followed by in the 1950s when services to Wearhead and Tow Law were cut back. By 1968 freight services had also ceased so that all rail track had been lifted on the branches except for the Weardale branch and its limestone traffic which lasted another 25 years, and the branch to Darlington. These photographs show Bishop Auckland station in its heyday. In the next chapter the reader will see how demolition of the station facilities and new uses for the railway land north to Newton Cap viaduct has resulted in new roads, new commercial facilities and a significant alteration in the fabric of the town.

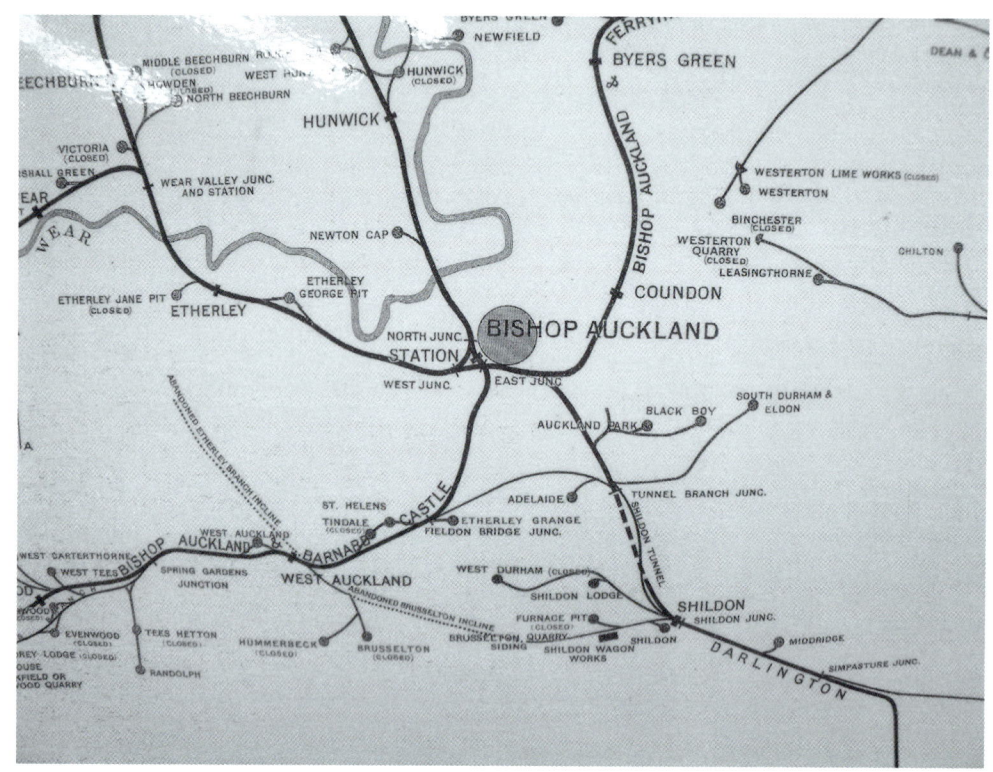

These two maps are complimentary to each other and show Bishop Auckland c. 1912 at the height of coal mining and railway development, and also owners of coal mining concessions in 1915.

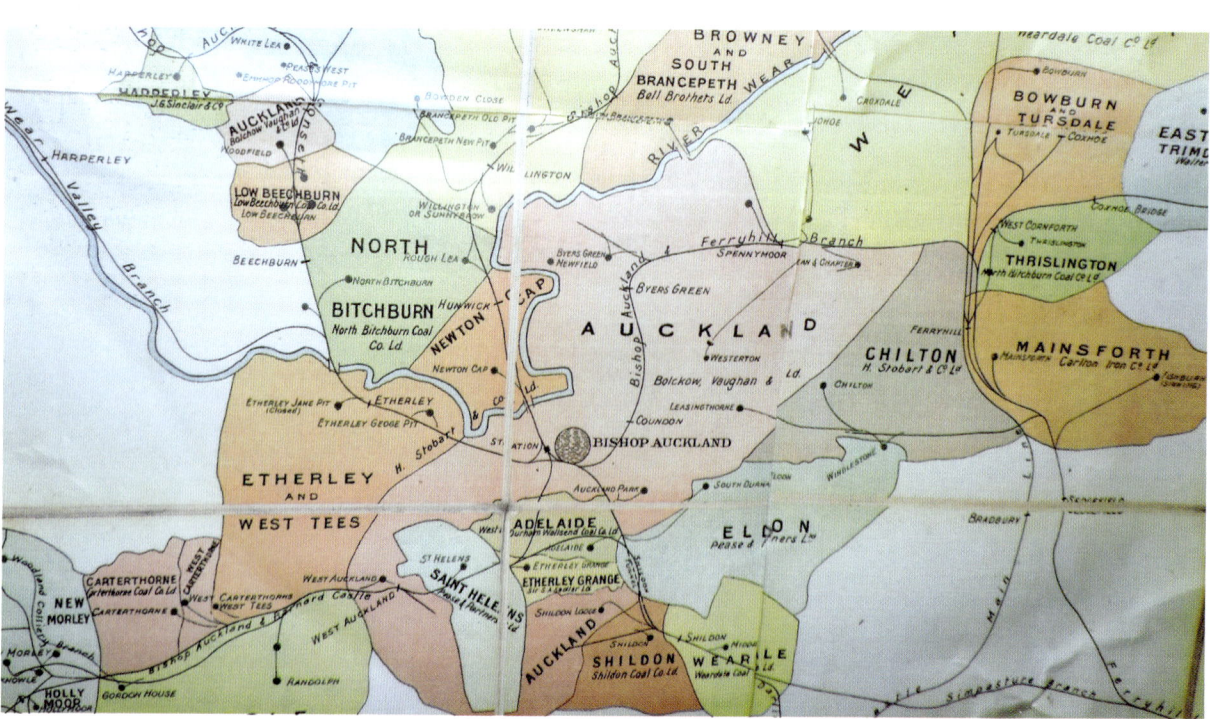

This, the oldest photograph, dates from c. 1910 and was taken from the station bridge approach, looking across platforms 2 and 3. There is a freight wagon in the loading dock next to platform 3 which was the platform for trains to Barnard Castle and Spennymoor. The two storey building had a restaurant on the ground floor and accommodation for the tenant of the refreshment room on the first floor. To the left is the site of the original Stockton & Darlington Railway station of 1842/3 which was rebuilt in 1856/7 when the North Eastern Railway branch to Durham opened. The station was then remodelled in 1866/67 when the new platform 2 to Durham opened. The original platform to the left of the two storey building became platform 1 serving trains to Darlington in one direction and Crook, Tow Law and Weardale in the other. The main entrance to the station was within the two storey building. On the right is the clock turret above the 1889 office building by platform 3. This platform had its own waiting rooms, booking office and direct entrance from the town. Also built was a covered footbridge over the four tracks to link with the rest of the station.

By 1953 the loading dock had been removed as this train for Barnard Castle leaves platform 3. On the left is Bishop Auckland East signal box which dates from the time of the previous c. 1910 picture. Note the four tracks through the station which allowed freight trains to pass stopping passenger services. The station bridge where photographs could be taken east, west and north-west above the railway complex was a favoured location, and still is.

This 22 May 1965 photograph by Ray Goad shows a V2 class locomotive no. 60884 on a Territorial Army troop train to Cheltenham at platform 3. The photograph from platform 2 shows the station bridge, east signal box and Albert Hill houses and nearer the covered footbridge that spanned the tracks – now reduced to two compared to the previous photograph.

The scene today with Albert Hill and new station bridge being the location guide. This picture was taken early one Sunday morning to minimise the effects of the ubiquitous motor vehicles.

A photograph that Mike Grantham took c. 1963 from the covered footbridge spanning platforms 2 and 3, looking towards the end of platform 1. The avoiding two tracks in the centre are out of use. Left middle is the east signal box in front of Cockton Hill and Escomb roads.

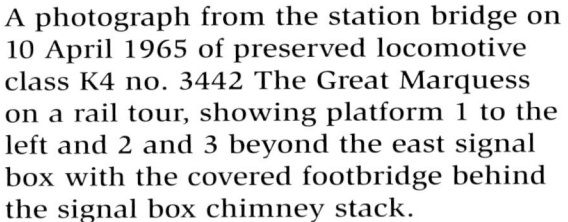

A photograph from the station bridge on 10 April 1965 of preserved locomotive class K4 no. 3442 The Great Marquess on a rail tour, showing platform 1 to the left and 2 and 3 beyond the east signal box with the covered footbridge behind the signal box chimney stack.

Compare the previous scene from this one in 1996 from a similar location. All the station paraphanalia has disappeared under car parks, B. & Q. and Halfords. The station is a single platform modern structure.

The rarely photographed platform 4 at Bishop Auckland railway station in its final form dating from 1905. This platform was used mainly for excursion traffic. Of greater importance to the 1950s trainspotters was that the mail train from Newcastle to the south stopped here every weekday for a couple of hours. Invariably the locomotive was a 'namer' or at least V2 or B1 classes – the most powerful locomotives seen on a daily basis. The triangular layout of the station was also used to allow newly built or serviced locomotives from North Road Works, Darlington to turn on the triangular layout and return to Darlington head-first. This 1962 photograph shows the railway scene just prior to the decline that occurred in the 1960s. The photograph was taken from the 1932 George Wright footbridge – that bridge also closed in 1966. However, the extensive signalling facilities are still complete. The tall building back left, originally belonging to the local Co-op, was in the hands of Ferens Brothers as an animal feeds manufacturing and storage base. The high north signal box controlling the goods station and line to Durham is back right. (c. Beamish Museum.)

The mail train in long gone days, c. 1962/63 taken from George Wright footbridge by Mike Grantham. Class A1 no. 60150 Willbrook stands at platform 4. Behind are the short loading docks. Behind the parcels office extreme left is the main entrance and platform 1.

Another Mike Grantham photograph of a rail tour on 28 September 1963 pulling into platform 4 behind Q7 class no. 63460. Beyond are the ends of platforms 2 and 3 and further back is Hanratty's scrapyard and the goods station, with the tower of the Wesleyan Church (four clocks) on the extreme right.

That scene today. Impossible to replicate exactly as the Morrison's supermarket building blots out the old sights, so this photograph was taken from further north to allow the 'Four Clocks' tower to be visible.

A 1960s photograph looking east along platform 1. Note that the platform is set at an angle (slightly north) in relation to the bridge over Newgate Street in the distance. The track in the foreground then curves to join the through lines. Houses in Albert Hill are on the right.

The station platform today and the rebuilt road bridge behind. The platform has been moved nearer the bridge and also extends about a meter south.

Three more photographs from the early 1960s. Firstly, looking south with platforms 2, 3 and 4 visible. Two tracks between platforms 2 and 3 have been removed; signals and water tower remain, and wagons are stored on the right. In the distance is the hospital in Escomb Road. The second photograph shows the veranda fronting the offices, booking hall and main entrance. On the extreme left is the covered walkway down from the approach road. Above the end of that walkway can be seen the covered footbridge spanning platforms 2 and 3.

The third photograph was taken from near the west signal box. On the left is the western end of platform 4 and the diesel rail car peeping out of the canopy over platform 1. In the middle are the loading docks and behind them the institute building. The main buildings on platforms 1 and 2 were demolished in 1981, although part of the building on platform 3 survived for a few more years when the Darlington service was moved to that platform – more convenient for the town centre. Trains moved back to the rebuilt platform 1 in 1987 when the current bungalow station building opened.

Right: A small part of the old platform 1 shown in the previous photograph is visible in this 2015 photograph at the western end of the new platform.

To complete this chapter on the railway station are modern photographs taken by Bishop Trains and Dave Calcutt in the last three years of traffic on the railway. On 12 July 2012 Prince Charles visited Auckland Castle and alighted from his train which was pulled by class A1 no. 60163 Tornado. The second photograph is of class A4 no. 60009 Union of South Africa on a rail tour returning from Stanhope on 15 May 2013. The last two photographs are of coal trains which ran from Wolsingham to Ratcliffe power station, Nottinghamshire or TATA steelworks, Scunthorpe from 4 July 2011 to 2 October 2013. On 12 July 2013 the train was double-headed by class 66 locomotives nos. 66848 and 66849 'Wylam Dilly' because of a locomotive failure the previous day and on 27 September 2013 locomotive class 56, no. 56312 'Jeremiah Dixon' is heading a train of coal empties to York.

Left: Tornado at platform 1 with many admirers taking photographs (BT).

Union of South Africa returning from Stanhope passing the station on the avoiding line (DC).

Above: The double-headed coal train from Wolsingham on the avoiding line (BT).

Right: Only a few days before the service ceased 'Jeremiah Dixon' pulling the coal empties (BT).

DEMOLITION AND RECONSTRUCTION

During the late 1980s and early 1990s the west side of the central area of Bishop Auckland town centre underwent dramatic changes when the closed railway line to Durham and the railway facilities based on the passenger and goods stations were swept away in order to build roads and new shopping areas. These changes extended south from the railway viaduct to the remaining railway line running east to west parallel to Escomb Road. These changes can be seen on the two maps. Fortunately, the late Ian McClen took many photographs in those years and a number of them are shown in the following pages.

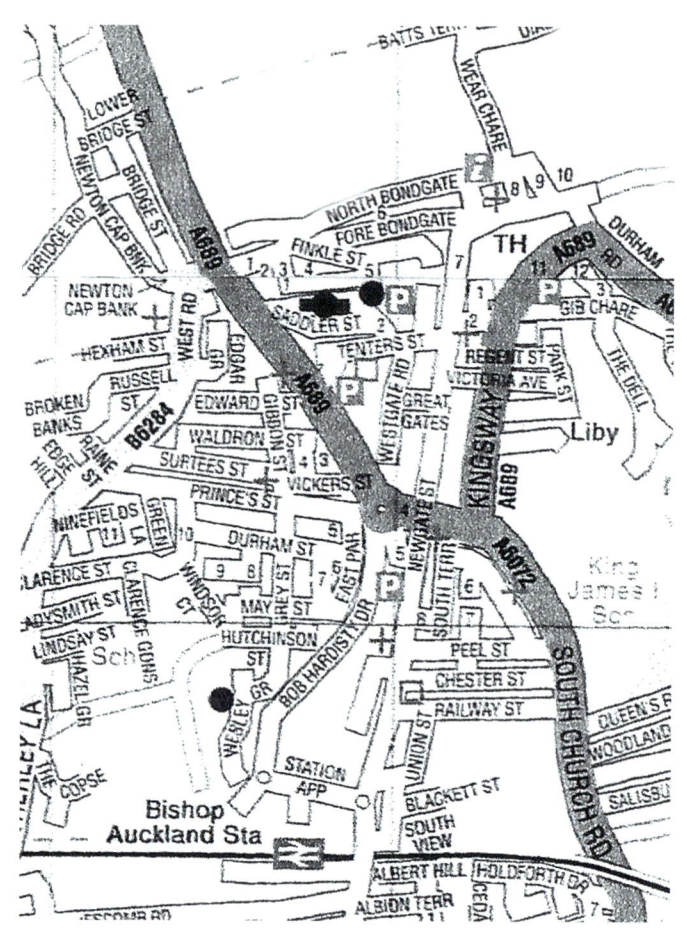

Maps, c. 1960 and 2000.

Tenters Street road bridge over the railway, c. 1963. The Odeon cinema in the background.

Tenters Street pedestrian bridge over the road in 2015, with the ugly civil service building at the back.

70

The conversion of the old railway viaduct to a two lane road started in September 1993 and took nearly two years to complete. This first photograph from the top of Bridge Street shows scaffolding on part of the railway arches and embankment work at both ends. This crane and a second one were a feature on the landscape for many months. Temporary coffer dams were built round the piers of the viaduct as part of close scrutiny of all parts of the bridge in order for strengthening of any parts where appropriate. A long view from the east shows the embankment work at the Toronto end of the bridge and the building of the road by-passing Toronto.

These two photographs show the old railway embankment on the south side was completely removed, and that reinforced concrete slabs were placed on top of the stone viaduct deck to provide a new road surface 13 feet wider than the railway to accommodate a two-way road with a footpath on either side. In the conversion, 4310 metres of concrete and 758 tonnes of steel were utilised. The concrete slabs also created a weather-seal roof over the 140 year structure.

Other very notable alterations were on the south side of the bridge where the northern portal of Bondgate Tunnel was filled with concrete as part of the building of the road approach on to the bridge. Also as part of the road changes railway cottages above the tunnel were demolished.

Road works in High Bondgate where a round-a-bout had been opened to allow traffic from the new Bob Hardisty Drive to travel east or west. The cottages above the railway tunnel had been demolished as one can see behind the temporary fencing. Bondgate Tunnel was located under the line of the round-a-bout.

The north end of Bob Hardisty Drive under construction with the new bus station off to the right behind this near building. In the distance is the gap in the buildings where the rebuilding of the viaduct would be under way ten years later.

The new round-a-bout completed in this photograph from 28 May 1984

The bus station under construction behind the new Newgate Centre. This work was designed to allow travellers to alight from the bus station and walk safely through the Newgate Centre into Newgate Street. Initially, the location of the Asda supermarket in the Centre attracted visitors, but when they moved out and Morrisons opened their store on former railway land further south, the volume of people using the Newgate Centre dropped – and all this before the retail developments at Tindale over the last decade. Left is the pointed roof facade of the 16th century Bay Horse Inn.

The bus station in May 1984 covering the demolished 19th century terraced housing of Saddler, Clayton, Grainger, Thompson and George streets. Houses at the north end of Etherley Lane are in the background.

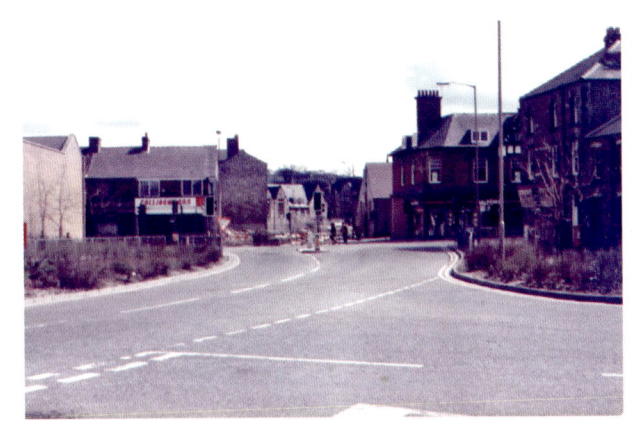

Again in May 1984 the remodelled junction of Newgate Street, Princes Street and the new road Bob Hardisty Drive on the line of the old railway north to Durham. The photograph looking east towards the old St Anne's School shows more road works in South Church Road at its junction with Newgate Street.

Two years later in the autumn of 1986 more road works occurred at the bottom of Princes Street when a round-a-bout was constructed to facilitate the extension of Bob Hardisty Drive southwards towards the former passenger and goods railway stations which were being demolished to allow the building of a new Morrisons superstore and other retail facilities.

By October 1986 the buildings on the former platform three of the railway station were out of use and the new road system was under way. In the background appears the skeleton scaffolding for the Morrisons superstore.

The new station building was well on its way to completion in November 1986 as Ian took this photograph from the Newgate Street bridge. The old platform three building and former railway institute building – later Edkins sales rooms - remain for a while longer.

The skeleton of Morrisons superstore in October 1986. The old railway goods station in the background. It was not demolished until summer 1990.

The store's appearance by June 1987.

The following four photographs, the rail ones taken by Ray Goad, seem to exemplify the major changes in Bishop Auckland in the past 50 years. On 8 April 1965 class K1 locomotive no. 62048 is approaching Tenters Street bridge from the south.

That same scene taken by Keith Cockerill in summer 2005 from the replacement pedestrian bridge shows Bob Hardisty Drive to the south. The houses on the right helped locate this picture as exact as possible compared to the previous one.

From Tenters Street road bridge in 1968 looking north, only a short while before the railway closed. Steam has been replaced by diesel traction. The line of the tunnel, gently curving right, can be seen where the large tree fills the gap between the houses in High Bondgate back centre. The tunnel was only a few feet below street level.

The same scene in summer 2005. The houses at right back helped Keith line up the shot. Off to the right is the bus station.

From 1984 to 1987 the Bishop Auckland by-pass east and south of the town was under construction, and this photograph is from February 1985 when the River Gaunless had been temporarily diverted to allow a tunnel for the river to be built on the line of the road. The straightening of the River Gaunless between South Church and Tindale Crescent as part of the by-pass project was partly responsible for floods in South Church in 2000, but that is another story.

The by-pass took through traffic away from South Church and St. Andrew's Road. This February 1987 photograph shows the road bed being laid down from Canney Hill to its junction with South Church Road. The bridge carries the railway between the town and Shildon.

May 1987 - the pedestrian bridge from North End Gardens to St. Andrew's Church graveyard. In the background are the houses in St. Andrew's Road.

This July 1989 picture shows the mobile crane putting the pedestrian bridge deck in place.

Building demolition and reconstruction also took place in the Market Place between 1989 and 1991 as can be seen on these photographs. First the demolition of the old Red Stamp Stores later Hardy & Co. (furnishers) building early in 1989 and its replacement by a new building for Iceland in 1990. On the right is Hintons supermarket.

Then the demolition of the old building between the Kings Arms and Harveys night club occurred in 1990. Harveys (now Monaco) had already replaced the building housing the former Angel Inn. This new building housed the job centre. The Queens Arms and Kings Head were still open for business.

From late 1991 until 1993 the Town Hall was also refurbished and altered internally, and part of the Market Square re-modelled – only to be remodelled again 20 years later. On the right of one of these 1992 photographs is the Castle Hotel – apparently boarded up.

This photograph dates from 2002 and shows the pedestrianised Market Square. The pedestrianised area was altered again ten years after in order to increase space between the front of the Town Hall, church and road. New street furniture has been provided including lighting, seats and trees. The photograph on the front cover shows the scene today.

The mid 1990s brought about the closure of Wilson's Forge east of Newgate Street and north of the railway. This foundry and engineering works was developed on part of the area formerly occupied by the Auckland Ironworks which had opened in 1863 and had closed in 1877. The site was acquired by Robert Wilson & Sons in the 1880s, though the business was originally established in 1842. It later acquired the premises of Lingford, Gardiner & Co., railway engineers and locomotive repairers, which went into liquidation in 1931. The company had been reconstituted in 1929 as Wilsons Forge (1929) Ltd. and continued trading successfully until comparatively recently. In the summer of 2000 permission was granted for the building of a new Asda supermarket on the site. This photograph dates from 1963.

This photograph from Ian McClen shows the derelict forge site prior to demolition in 2001. Vandalised offices mid right.

Skeletal remains of the foundry in the background whilst development work takes place on the office site and to its rear in 2001.

Ian's view reproduced today.

MEMORABILIA OF BISHOP AUCKLAND

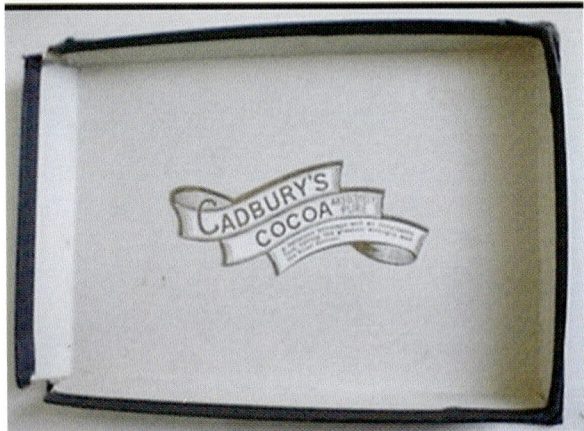

Cadbury's cocoa box with a picture of the railway viaduct on the top.

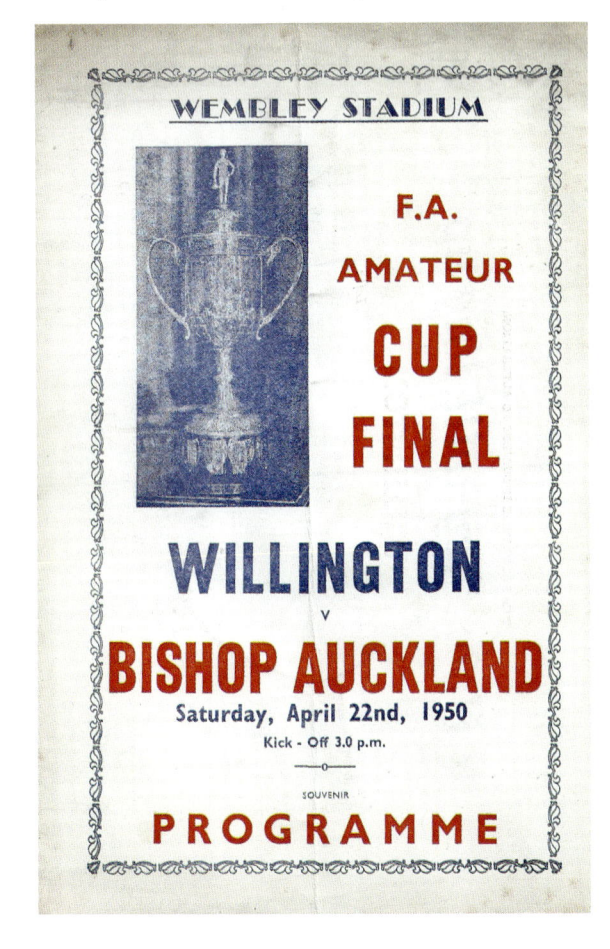

An S.S. Lingford & Co. dish.

A 1902 Edward VII and Queen Alexandra Coronation picture from Robert Walburn, tailor and hatter, 6-7 Newgate Street.

Left: Programme for the 1950 F.A. Amateur Cup Final between Willington and Bishop Auckland. I shall gloss over the result somewhat, but Bishop lost 4-0. The club had to wait four years before the glorious hat trick of 1955 to 57, and two more Wembley defeats in the meantime!

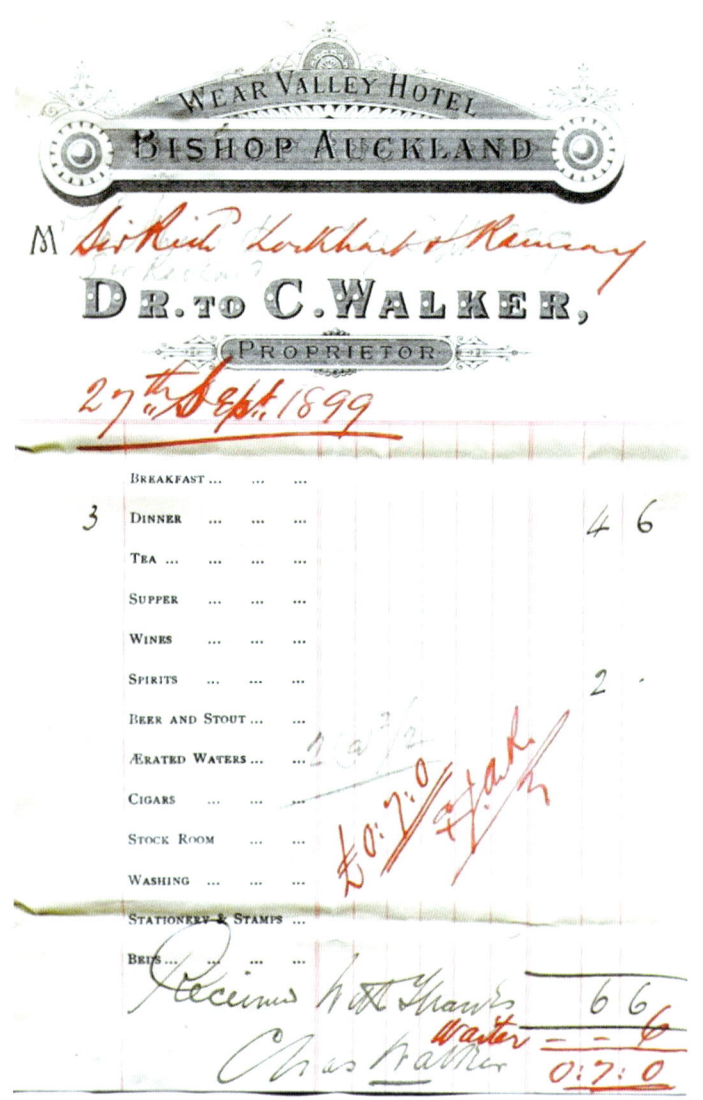

A Wear Valley Hotel bill of 1899 for three dinners and spirits for 7 shillings, with sixpence tip for the waiter.

A certificate from British Railways awarding Bishop Auckland station second prize in the best kept station competition of 1953.

Right: A bottle from Sant & Son, mineral water manufacturers. Mr. Sant was also the managing director of the Hippodrome when it opened in 1909 offering " healthy entertainment, free of vulgarity."

Left: Two much more decorative pieces of china with greetings from Bishop Auckland.

Four comic postcards from 1900 to 1920 promoting Bishop Auckland. Cynicus, real name Martin Anderson, was a popular caricaturist in an age when society was far more class conscious than today. He set up his own publishing company in c. 1902 and continued into World War One. As can be seen the cards could be overprinted with any place name – a good selling gimmick – and the two illustrated have the church and railway connection. The other two cards are more of the traditional greetings variety really saying how good it is in Bishop Auckland.

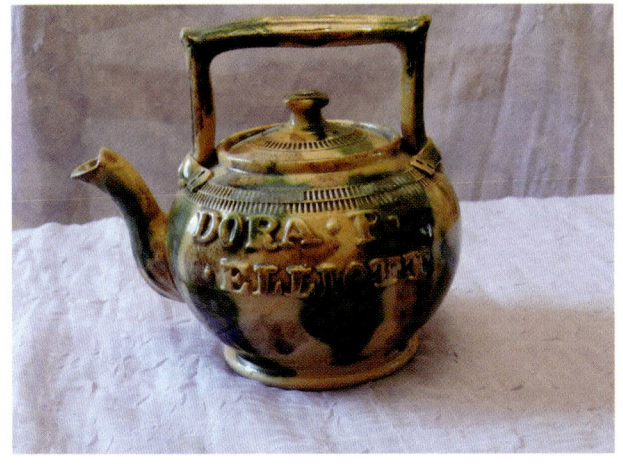

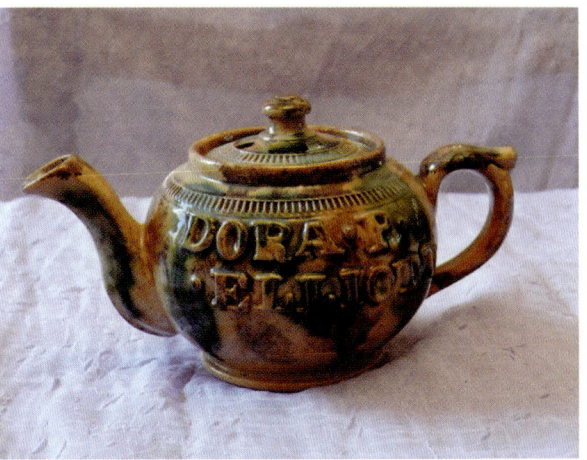

Two pieces of pottery from Canney Hill Pottery. The kettle and teapot, both inscribed 'Dora P. Elliott.'

83

China salt & pepper pots and sugar bowl.

A Communion token from 1867. The rest of the inscription says "Revd. Thos. Boyd. U. P. Congregation. Bishop Auckland. Revd. Boyd was the minister at the United Presbyterian Church in South Church Lane (Road).

Another present from Bishop Auckland in the shape of this china cup.

Left: The British Railways poster advertising the three overnight trains on Friday 21 April 1950 to London Marylebone at a fare of 36 shillings (£1.80) return for the journey which took over seven hours each way. I remember a similar journey three years later when you spent the morning wandering around London, including the usual visit and photograph (if you had a camera) outside Buckingham Palace railings.

ANCIENT & MODERN

Many inhabitants of Bishop Auckland will remember Farr's Yard which was situated between William Street and George Street in the north west of the town. Thomas Farr who was born in Haverill, Suffolk c. 1853 came to Bishop Auckland in the 1870s and married Elizabeth Priestman in about 1875. His address is recorded as the Sawmills, Pollards Lands in the town in the 1881 census. He was a coach builder. The 1st edition of the Ordnance Survey in 1857 shows a large timber yard stretching from the rear of Bondgate south to where Tenters Street was being built, and bounded by Wood Street in the east and a park area sited next to George Street in the west. Presumably there was some sort of dwelling in the timber yard. The Farrs lived at 1 Wood Street at the next two censuses in 1891 and 1901, and lived at 1 William Street by 1911 – five bedroomed house which existed until the Newgate Centre was built in the early 1980s. Domestically, the Farrs had a grief-ridden life as all of their five children had died by the 1911 census.

However, from a business point of view Thomas was very successful. An account of the town published c. 1894 says this about Mr. Farr, "coach building – Mr. Farr has no reason to fear comparison with any of his competitors in this line of business ... his extensive and well equipped works ... forty hands being regularly employed ... making landaus, broughams, barouches, phaetons, waggonettes ... charges are moderate ... excellent quality of his work." Advertisements from c. 1894 give a picture of the business on site – coachbuilding, painting and shoeing forge.

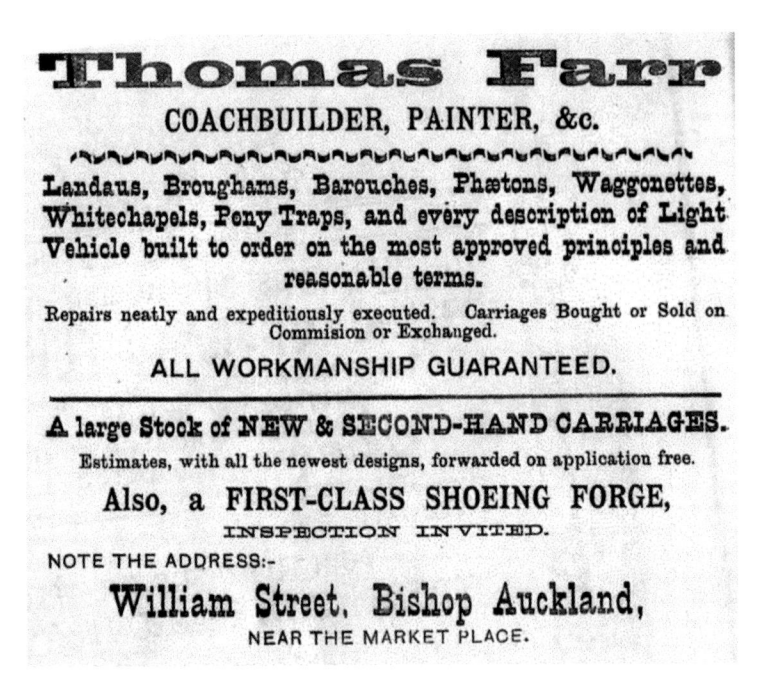

Two 1890s advertisements for Mr. Farr's business.

The business continued well into the 20th century and Farr's coachbuilders appeared in Kelly's Trade Directory as late as 1925 though Thomas would have been over 70 by then. However, the introduction of the motor vehicle in the early 20th century no doubt had a major impact on his business. By 1897 the adjacent area to the west of the coach-building business had also changed in that an auction mart was present on part of the open park site mentioned above. By 1920 houses had been built on the east side of George Street and there were buildings behind Wood Street covering the southern end of the yard. Thomas and his wife Elizabeth continued to live in William Street until she died in 1937 and he died in 1940.

The use of Farr's Yard did change. As an example a bus timetable from the Coronation brochure of 1937 shows a Favourite Direct Service Ltd timetable and advertisement for Coronation Day, and presumably buses were based at the Yard. In the 1950s it seems the yard was also used as a vehicle depot by Brunskills heavy haulage but by then the auction mart had disappeared and the Ministry of Pensions & National Insurance had offices on the north east of the site.

FAVOURITE DIRECT SERVICE, LTD.

The only Direct Service to Stockton & Middlesbrough

Buses leave Bishop Auckland Market Place
Five Minutes past every hour.

Ask the Conductor for a complete Time Table - FREE.

WEDNESDAY, MAY 12th - - CORONATION DAY—

SEDGEFIELD RACES: Special Buses will leave the Market Place direct for the Race Course at 1-5 p.m.

Let us quote for the conveyance of your Private Party.
Modern Saloons may be hired for journeys of any distance.

FOR QUOTATIONS WRITE:
FAVOURITE DIRECT SERVICE, LTD.,
FARR'S YARD, GEORGE ST., BISHOP AUCKLAND.
'Phone 271.

Left: Favourite bus company advertisement from 1937. Their address was Farr's Yard, George Street and they had an early telephone number – 271.

Below: Is this one of Mr. Farr's carriages? A photograph from over 100 years ago taken at the north end of the Skirlaw bridge over the River Wear at Newton Cap.

The demise of horse-drawn transport was hastened by the introduction of the motor vehicle and in looking at freight transport in Bishop Auckland today it is appropriate to look at Ingram's Remover & Storers who were set up in the 1950s by Bill Ingram who started off part-time as a carton merchant along with carrying out local house moves and deliveries for friends and neighbours. The company later went into the express delivery business as well as Royal Mail parcel deliveries so that by the late 1970s the company changed their name to Ingram's Removers & Storers.

In the early days Ingrams maintained their own vehicles, and this Ford Capri with its unique pick-up body was used by the maintenance Dept.

Right: Another vehicle from the 1970s, a Bedford. Suitable for domestic removals.

Eventually, the haulage side of the business was phased out and the company concentrated on removals and storage. By that time the company had moved into their present premises in Percy and Morland streets (former United bus company premises). In the 1990s the company expanded their commercial removal business and in the last decade the storage of public and private sector document archives has become a feature. In 2010 a new depot for documentation record management was opened at South Church Enterprise Park. Bill died in 1995 and the firm is now run by his sons Ian and Malcolm.

Bedford and Ford vans were the mainstays of the fleet, but by the 1990s the superior Mercedes Benz vehicles (shown below) were introduced. At about that time vehicle maintenance was transferred to a local Mercedes dealer.

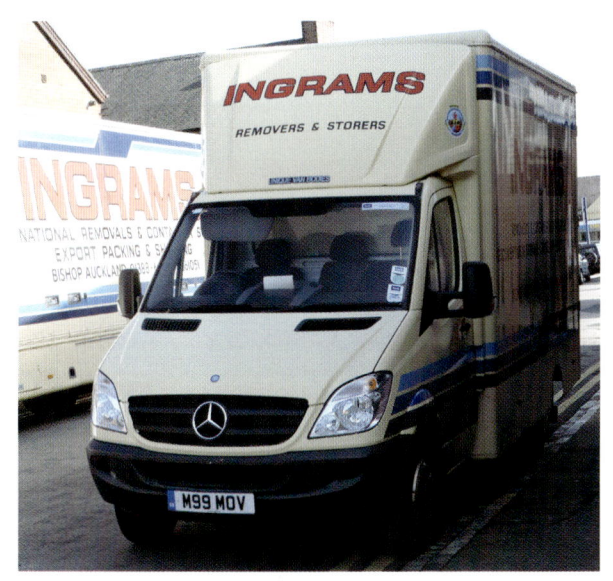

A 2015 photograph of one of the smaller Mercedes vehicles which still have a role in domestic moves and also as feeders to the larger vehicles when access to customers premises may be difficult.

This 2015 Mercedes Benz vehicle is the latest addition to the fleet. It is purpose built to meet London's strict exhaust emissions, negotiate narrow roads, and has a carrying capacity of 1200 tonnes and volume capacity of 1500 cu. feet.

The fleet in 2014 at the new depot in South Church Enterprise Park.

Acknowledgements

Auckland Castle Trust, Beamish – The North of England Open Air Museum, Bishop Trains, John Askwith, Keith Brown, David Calcutt, George & Linda Campbell, Margaret Carney, F. M. Carr, Keith Cockerill, Marjorie Cook, Wilf Dixon, Ray Goad, Mike Grantham, Brian Hayward, Valerie Hetherington, Mel Holmes, Ian & Malcolm Ingram, the late Ian McClen, George Nairn, John Rusby, Tom Sellars.

Thanks also for the layout and technical input from Andrew Clark.

The O.S. maps reproduced by kind permission of the Ordnance Survey.

Bibliography

History & Characteristics of Bishop Auckland – Matthew Richley
History of Bishop Auckland – Tom Hutchinson
The Changing Face of Bishop Auckland – Barbara Laurie
Trade Directories/Gazetteers, 1827 – 1938
Censuses 1841 - 1911
Reference Material in Town Hall Library, Bishop Auckland

St. Anne's C. of E. Primary School 1998, year 6. Back left: Christopher English, Michael Kelly, Louis Quinn, David Sixsmith, Robert Bowron, Alex Grayson. Third row left: Hemish Dissanayake, Damian Kandish, David Jackson, Jonathan Greenwood, Robert Hall, Duane Wardman, Aaron Miller. Second row left: Paul Bake, Rebecca Daniels, Nicola Gaines, Rachel Elstob, Jamie Dawes, Mary Deacon, Lisa Bestford, Anthony Peacock. Front left: Charlotte Holmes, Laura Campbell, Stephanie Cooke, Kate Marshall, Miss L. Chapman, Helen Aspinall, Katherine Douthwaite, Kim Wilson, Ashley Robinson.

Back cover: A Lingfords' Advertisement from 1946.